ERNIE

A Photographer's Memoir

TONY MENDOZA

Introduction by Owen Edwards

Capra Press / 1985

LIBRARY OF CONGRESS CATALOGING IN PUBLICATION DATA
Mendoza, Tony, 1941–
ERNIE: A PHOTOGRAPHER'S MEMOIR
1. Photography of cats.   I. Title.
TR729.C3M46   1985   770'.92'4   85-11313
ISBN 0-88496-240-7 (pbk.)

Capra Press
Post Office Box 2068
Santa Barbara, Ca. 93120

The Man in The Cat and The Cat in The Man

OWEN EDWARDS

The wisdom of many aboriginal cultures teaches that all human beings possess a bush soul, an equivalent being in nature to which the possessor feels a powerful spiritual connection. This soul can be an animal, a plant, even a particular part of the landscape, and many primitive rites of passage are intended to reveal to the initiate his natural equivalent.

Some perceptive characters manage to recognize their bush souls despite the distractions of modern society. One such fortunate biped is Tony Mendoza, an architect-turned-photographer who walked into a Manhattan loft once upon a time and met a cat named Ernie. Was there instant recognition that a cat shared a soul with this particular man? No outsider can know, and Mendoza isn't talking. But the pictures that came of their two-year-long liaison are not the pictures a man would make of a cat; they are the pictures a cat would make of a cat. Of course, anyone who knows anything about cats knows that cats are too sublimely centered on the universe of themselves *ever* to *take* photographs of another cat. So, if Mendoza (the human version) or his editors had really understood what I (and now you) understand, they would have called this book "Portrait of The Artist As A Young Cat."

When I arrived in New York City, determined to turn my talent into fame and fortune, I had a carload full of photographic equipment, a trunkload of dreams, and no place to stay. I started putting up ads all over downtown Manhattan.

One day, I noticed someone else's ad: "A painter wishes to share her darkroom equipped loft with another artist."

I rushed to the nearest phone.

Nancy and I need a roommate; the rents on these lofts are criminal. So bring someone in, someone who can pay a little rent money and operate a can opener. Someone who knows his place.

Nancy's a painter with very good taste. For example, she chose me.

I'm Ernie.

A woman's voice answered: "Hello."

"Hello. My name is Tony Mendoza. I saw your ad."

"I hope you're not allergic to cats."

"No. Do you have a cat?"

"Do I ever!"

So this guy shows up and we interview him.

I know he's right the minute he walks in. His socks are delicious. I grab on and hug his ankle to my belly, till Nancy has to pull me off.

He tells Nancy what a handsome cat I am. Says he wants to take pictures of me.

My mind is made up. Now it's time to turn on the charm. I bring out my plastic golf ball and bat it around the loft for a little noise. Then I do the tail-chase for a few minutes—that always gets a laugh—then I settle down to chew lovingly on Elephant.

I've got him hooked.

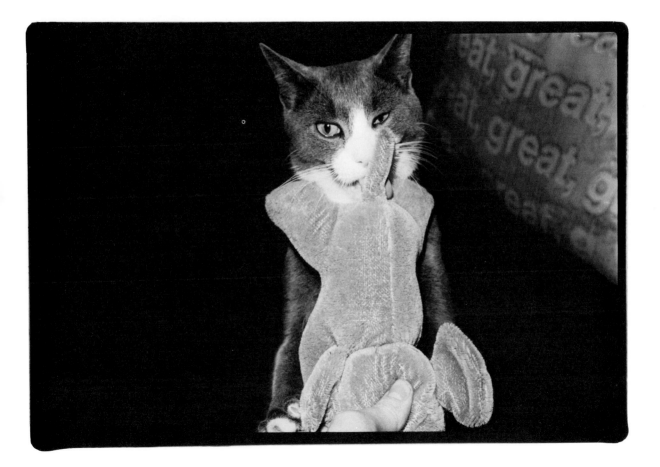

The new guy's got some strange habits.

Now that he's moved in, he spends a lot of time down on all fours, crawling after me. Every time I wake up from a nap, there he is, two inches away from my face, clicking that box at me. It used to be more private around here.

I moved in and pretty soon I was photographing Ernie every day. Ernie's grey markings were perfect for black and white photography. But it was his personality and his activity that made him a great model.

I preferred taking pictures from Ernie's eye-level, even if it meant crawling around the loft for hours at a time.

But that's not all. He talks to me in this God-awful high voice humans use on children and pets. All day long it's:

"Over here, Ernito. You look so beautiful today. Come on, Erniti. Ernititi. Give me a smile. Beautiful. Hold it! Now let's try something more animal. A little more fang. Beautiful!"

Brother.

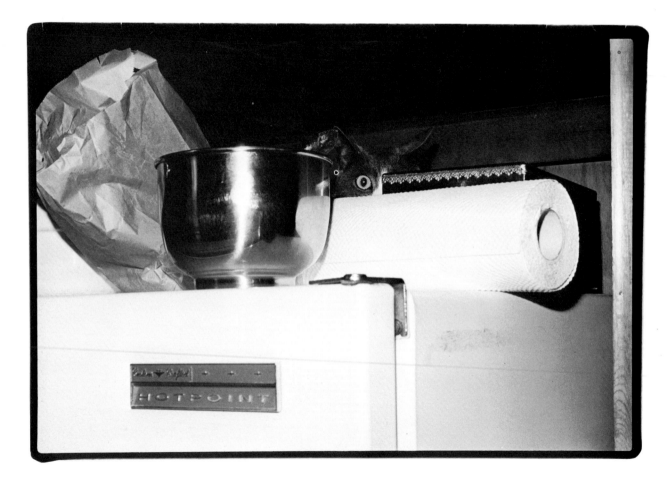

Ernie was a born predator. Maybe a part of him still longed for his ancestral jungle home. Every morning he would go out on the roof outside the kitchen window and stalk the pigeons who sat on the edge.

He did this every morning for two years, and he never got any closer than ten feet.

Well, I was never too serious about the pigeons. Have you ever wanted to eat a New York City pigeon? Now I have nothing against some of the smaller, tastier morsels.

He was at his best with insects. He could snag a dragonfly midflight. In fact, he kept our loft so bug-free that I occasionally had to import a cockroach to give Ernie something to practice on.

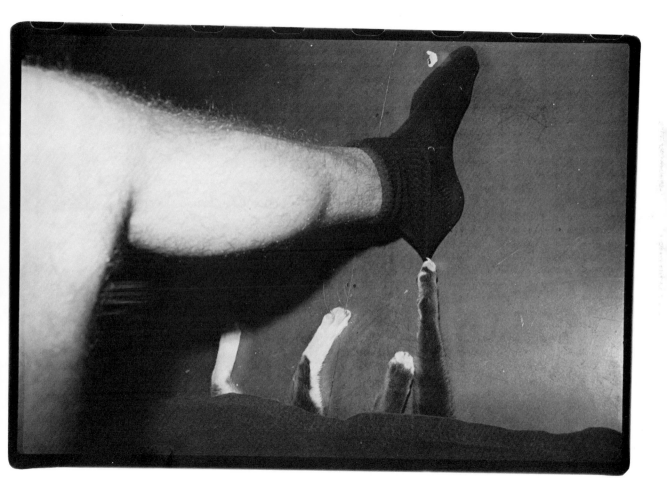

We're going to have to have a little talk.

When he brings home a cockroach for me to deal with, that's one thing. I go along. It's not what I would prefer, but it pays to keep your hand in.

But then he brings home this stray cat! That's where I draw the line. This is my home we are talking about. Please.

I won't even mention the time with the dog.

We have an understanding: I'm no cuddly, cutie-pie cat. There are plenty of those around—posing for birthday cards and calendars.

Basically, I'm fierce, and he knows it.

We had this game: "Hand Combat."

I would place my left hand on the back of the couch and Ernie would try to get it (while I took pictures of Ernie in mid-air with my right hand).

Nobody ever warned me that photography was a dangerous occupation. For two years I wore battle scars on my left hand.

Most of the time, though, Ernie kept busy just being a cat.

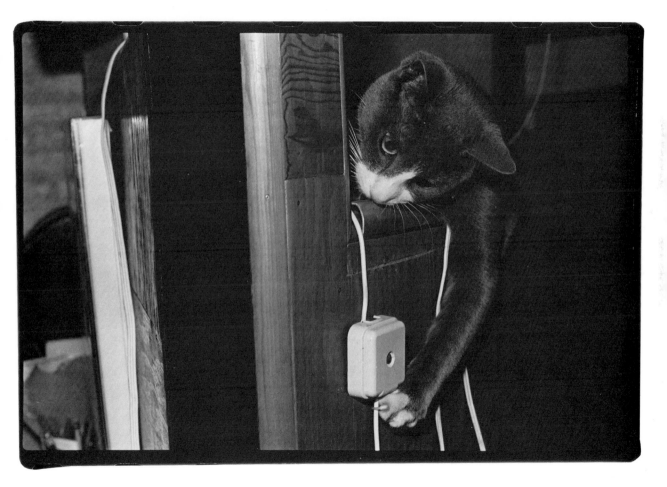

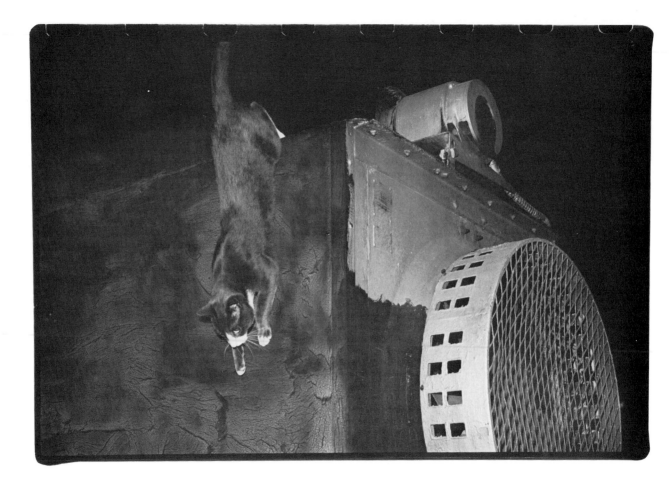

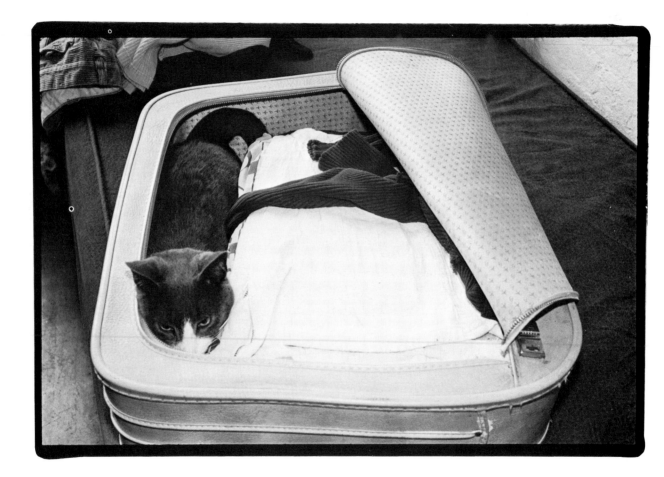

I have a lot more to do now that I'm a photographer's assistant. I help him look at pictures. I pose. I retrieve Elephant whenever he throws him up on the darkroom roof. (We've got to have a talk about that routine. Elephant belongs next to me, at all times.)

Sometimes I have to help him in the darkroom. He doesn't see so well in the dark. (That's probably how he got started washing his prints in a sandbox.)

Ordinarily, I don't quarrel with his subject matter. But every now and then he blows it.

After I had lived in the loft for one year, I had accumulated five thousand negatives of Ernie and a growing list of debts to credit cards and relatives. I realized I had to sell some pictures and make some money. I put together a commercial portfolio—which had become increasingly filled with cat pictures—and took it around to art directors.

After a while, a downtown newspaper called and asked me to do a cat cover. I wanted to use Ernie, but was voted down by an editor who insisted on using her own cat instead.

The results got mixed reviews.

Ernie started catching on, though. American and European photography magazines published selections. Three postcard companies Ernied some postcards. Two museums bought Ernie pictures.

I had a one-man, one-cat show. My father came to the show.

"I see you've become a cat photographer."

"I guess so."

"You're crazy. If you want to make money, you should be taking pictures of beautiful women."

"You're probably right, Pop. But in the meantime, I think I'll do a book of Ernie photographs."

"An Ernie book? Good luck."

Celebrity has not spoiled me.

Postcards, magazines, even a book . . . it's just part of the job.

Besides, you can't get far in the print media anyway. My agent has other ideas. We're talking film, talking TV. I hear Stephen King has a script about a haunted cat. . . .

After living in the loft for two years, I moved out. I just couldn't afford Manhattan rents doing cat photography. So I moved to Brooklyn, where my sister lived in her brownstone with Jaime, her one-year-old son. Jaime became my next project, and soon I was crawling all over the floor again.

All of a sudden, one day there's all this activity: loud strangers tearing up the place. I stay out on the roof till the storm's over.

And the next day he's gone. He doesn't come back that night.

He's gone the day after that, too.

EPILOGUE

He came to visit once.
    So?
I suppose he expected me to chew on his socks.
Maybe I was supposed to chase a bug. Be cute. Bare my fangs.
Just like old times.
I ignored him of course.
Now I hear he's closed the deal on that Ernie book.
So far I've heard no mention of any percentage points for old Ernie.

For some reason, I didn't go back to visit Nancy and Ernie till a year later. I went up to him and made a big fuss, but he just looked at me blankly and walked away.

But later, after talking with Nancy for a while, I saw him eyeing me curiously. I casually scratched the back of the couch.

He casually sauntered to the front of the couch....

Crouched...and sprang.

About the Photographer

Tony Mendoza was born in Havana, Cuba, in 1941. He bought his first camera at age eleven and continued photographing through grammar school, high school, Yale University (Bachelor of Engineering), and the Harvard Graduate School of Design (Master of Architecture).

In 1973, to the dismay of his relatives and creditors, he turned full time to the pursuit of photography as art.

Since then, his work has been exhibited and published widely. He has received numerous awards, including a National Endowment for the Arts Photography Fellowship in 1981, and a New York Foundation for the Arts Photography Fellowship and a Guggenheim Photography Fellowship, both in 1985.

His photographs are in the collections of various museums, including the Museum of Fine Arts in Boston and the Museum of Modern Art in New York.